Michael Rosen

No Breathing
in Class

Illustrated by Korky Paul

PUFFIN BOOKS

PUFFIN BOOKS

Published by the Penguin Group
Penguin Books Ltd, 80 Strand, London WC2R 0RL, England
Penguin Putnam Inc., 375 Hudson Street, New York, New York 10014, USA
Penguin Books Australia Ltd, 250 Camberwell Road, Camberwell, Victoria, Australia
Penguin Books Canada Ltd, 10 Alcorn Avenue, Toronto, Ontario, Canada M4V 3B2
Penguin Books (NZ) Ltd, Cnr Rosedale and Airborne Roads, Albany, Auckland,
New Zealand
Penguin Books (South Africa) (Pty) Ltd, 24 Sturdee Avenue, Rosebank 2196,
South Africa

Penguin Books Ltd, Registered Offices: 80 Strand, London WC2R 0RL, England

www.penguin.com

First published 2002
1 3 5 7 9 10 8 6 4 2

Printed in Hong Kong by Midas Printing Ltd

British Library Cataloguing in Publication Data
A CIP catalogue record for this book is available from the British Library

ISBN 0 141 30022 1

For Elsie – M. R.

To Barney White – K. P.

··· Contents ···

Unfair

When we went over the park
Sunday mornings
to play football
we picked up sides.

Lizzie was our striker
because she had the best shot.

When the teachers
chose the school team
Marshy was our striker.

Lizzie wasn't allowed to play,
they said.
So she watched us lose, instead …

Strict

Maybe you think you have a
teacher
who's really strict,
maybe you know a really strict
teacher.
But when I was at school
we had a teacher who was so strict
you weren't allowed to breathe in
her lessons.

That's true, we weren't allowed to
breathe.
It was really hard to get through
a whole day without breathing.
Lips tightly shut.
Face going red.
Eyeballs popping out.
She'd go round the class glaring at us
and then she'd suddenly catch sight of
one of us and she'd yell,

'NO BREATHING, DO YOU
HEAR ME? NO BREATHING.'
And you had to stop breathing
right away.
The naughty ones used to try and
take quick secret breaths
under the table.
They'd duck down where she
couldn't see them

snatch a quick breath and come
back up
with their mouth shut tight.
Then someone would say,
'Excuse me, miss, can I go outside
and do some breathing?'
And she'd say,

'WHAT? CAN'T YOU WAIT?
YOU'VE HAD ALL PLAYTIME
TO BREATHE, HAVEN'T YOU?'
And then she'd ask someone a
question
like, 'Where's Tibet?'
and someone'd put up their hand
and say, 'Er … it's –'
and she'd be right in there with:

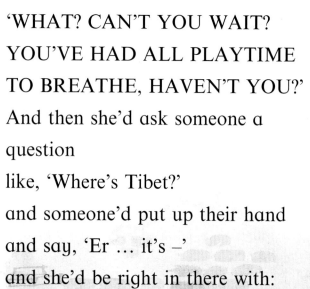

'YOU'RE BREATHING. I SAW
YOU BREATHE.'

'I wasn't, miss, really I wasn't.'

'WELL YOU ARE NOW, AREN'T
YOU?'

It was terrible.

She was so strict ...

Top Board

After three weeks of swimming
lessons
Mr Hicks the swimming teacher
said,
'OK, Michael, I want you to dive
off the top board.'

WHAT?!
Is he crazy? I can't do that.
The board is miles up in the air.
When people dive off there
they drop through the air
at a hundred miles an hour.

I've only ever dived off the
side before.
Just lean forward and flop.

'Up you go, lad, just pretend it's
the side and just go, lad, go,'
says Mr Hicks.

Up I go. I stand on the board ...

... the big clock at the other end of
the pool
is just the same height as me.
The paint is peeling off the ceiling.
It's hotter up here
and the air is full of shouting.
Underneath my feet it feels like
sandpaper ...

'… Just pretend it's the side
and just go, lad, go …'

So I did.
It felt like doing a handstand on
nothing.
It felt like my belly was going into
my legs.
When I hit the water
it was like someone walloping me in
the face.

'Well done,' said Mr Hicks.
'I want five more of those before the
end of the lesson.'

15

The Register

Right Class 6
register time –
that means everyone sitting down.
Everyone, Darren.
No, Darren, we're not feeding the
snails now.
Sarah, could you pass me the
register?
No I haven't got it, you've got it.
You went to fetch it, remember?
Oh that was yesterday was it?

Darren, leave the snails alone.

One moment everyone,

Mr Hardware wants a word.

Right Class 6

Mr Hardware says that any tennis

balls landing

in the gutter by the kitchen will be

left there till Christmas

when they'll be sent to

Dr Barnardo's.

No, he's not my doctor, Louise
my doctor doesn't need tennis balls
Dr Barnardo's not alive he's –
I know, Wayne, that if he's not alive
he can't use the tennis balls.
Darren, don't touch the snails, do
you hear me?
Does anyone know who or what is
Dr Barnardo's?
No Hugh, not a dog's home.
Yes Abdul, a children's home,
well done.

I wonder, Mrs Morris –

I don't want to be rude –

but I'm just settling the children
down,

perhaps you could see a way to
leaving now,

mmm?

I'm sure David is OK, Mrs Morris.

Yes, cake-making on Friday will be
lovely, Mrs Morris,

but –

Wayne that is very rude.

We've talked about kissing before.

If Mrs Morris wants to kiss David

goodbye

that's OK and you've no right to

laugh at –

thank you again Mrs Morris, yes

biscuit-making too

That'll be lovely, thank you so much,

goodbye, Mrs Morris

she's not waving to you, Sophie.

Yes Colin?

Well, I'm sure Mr Hardware means
any kind of ball
footballs, basketballs.

You got a baseball from your
American cousin.

That was very nice of him.

No I don't know who won the
World Series.

I can't guess because I don't know
the names
of any of the baseball teams.

Ah – Mrs Riley, good morning.
Right, Class 6,
Mrs Riley says that if anyone who
usually has school dinner
on a Thursday but wants a school
packed lunch for the outing
to the Science Museum, then could
they fill in the form.

Yes, Judy?

The form.

Well, I'm not quite sure what form
for the moment,
but I'm sure a form will be coming
along soon.

They usually do.

And I'll tell you when it does.

Well, if you don't want a school
packed lunch
and you don't bring a packed lunch
then you'll be very hungry, won't
you?

Darren, I don't want to have to tell
you about the snails again
we're doing the register now, not
snails,
yes, Zoë I know quite well that I'm
not actually doing the
register
at this very second
but I will be
and I would be
and I could be …

Do you know what the time is,
Mervyn?
You do.
Do you know how many minutes
late you are, Mervyn?
You do.
Do you know why you're late every
morning, Mervyn?
You do.
Do you have any idea how we are
going to get you
to come to school on time, Mervyn?
You don't.

Mark and Hong are sitting very
nicely.
Ah Mrs Morris, you're back.
Yes, we could make toffee as well
an excellent idea …
Qui-et!
There'll be no toffee for anyone
if there's that kind of noise …
thank you so much Mrs Morris
I'm sure we have the right pans for
making toffee
but I can't look right now
bye bye yes of course, bye bye.

Rasheda, Jason, Simone all sitting
very nicely
Darren not sitting nicely.
Not sitting at all in fact.
Oh no he's left the lid off,
quick, Abdul
the lid
put the lid back on the snails.
What? One's missing.
Which one?
No not all of you.
Everyone come back,
sit down.

Abdul and just Abdul
can you tell us which snail is
missing?

Robin.

Was Robin in the aquarium before?
Darren?

No Mervyn, snails don't eat each
other.

You know they eat leaves.

All term we've been looking at how
they eat leaves
we've written poems about how they
eat leaves,
we've drawn graphs of how many
leaves they eat in a day
and now you're telling me that they
eat each other.
You know sometimes I wonder why
we've got these snails
here.

It really isn't anything to cry about
Paul.
I know Robin was your favourite
and I'm sure Batman doesn't miss
him.
I'm not sure snails do miss each
other.
Look, I don't want to deal with this
just now.
I'm sure Robin will turn up,
he can't have gone far.
Snails don't gallop do they?

Darren, is that the truth?

Is what Salima is saying true?

Is it?

Well, take Robin out of your pocket

right now,

put him back in the aquarium

and go straight downstairs to see

Mrs Rashid

and you can explain to her what

you did to Robin.

I'm not sure you'll be here for

Mrs Morris's baking day

at this rate.

Ah who's this?

John.

No, I'm sorry John you can't have
the register
just yet.

Tell Mrs Riley we'll be down with it
in just a moment.

Right Class 6.

The register.

Oh – where is it?

It was here just a moment ago.

Can anyone see the register?

Can anyone see the register?

I Think

I think
it's really bad news
they don't put paper
in our school loos.

If you need paper
you have to ask
right in front
of everyone in class.

You may think
I'm a bit of a fool
but that's why
I don't go to school.

Australia

They said I was a failure
when I couldn't spell Austrailure.
Now I can spell Australia
and they still say I'm a falia.

Mr Baggs

I was walking home from school
with Mr Baggs,
the teacher who took us for football
and he said:
'You see Michael, what we need in
the team
is a really good centre-half,
someone who can control the game
from midfield
collect the ball in the middle
distribute the ball to the front
players.
A good centre-half can turn a game.
He can make all the difference.
Now who have we got playing in
the middle?

– oh my goodness it's you
I forgot
I'm sorry
I wasn't thinking
no hard feelings, OK?

Scared

We were talking in the playground
one day
about who was the easiest scared.
I said I was scared of nothing,
'Just try me with a dare.'

There was talk of spiders and
graveyards at night,
tunnels and tigers and sharks,
jellyfish that sting as you swim in
the sea,
dogs that bite but don't bark.

I said I was scared of nothing at all,
'Nothing gives me a fright
even if I was locked in a room
and left there for one whole night.'

End of the day at the back of the
class,
everyone going home,
planned to stay the night at school,
going to do it on my own.

Watched the rest of the class walk
out,
see them shut the door.
I got myself under the table
face held close to the floor.

No one noticed I hadn't left,
the place was quiet and dark.
An aeroplane crossed the night-time
sky,
shouts came in from the park.

I said I was here to find myself:
was it true I'm never scared?
Now I was here all on my own
doing the daring dare.

41

My plan was to stay all night in the
room
and when the morning came
I'd be waiting for everyone there
looking just the same.

I walked about and looked at the
walls
the pictures and the noticeboard.
There was one of a hairy spider's
nest
and the head of a tiger that roared.

I turned my back on the pictures
looked out of the window instead.
What was that down there in the
yard?
A body without a head?

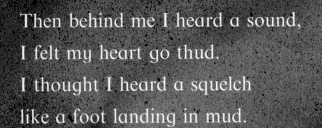

Then behind me I heard a sound,
I felt my heart go thud.
I thought I heard a squelch
like a foot landing in mud.

There was a creak from under the
table,
an eye blinked from the wall.
Far off down the corridor
I heard a cry from the hall.

44

Why had I done this stupid thing?
Did I have something to prove?
What was that noise over there?
The tables were beginning to move.

I screamed as loud as I could,
'Don't do it, please don't do it!'
If I was braver, I'd've just kept quiet
but that was the moment I blew it.

The lights went on and there were
my friends:
'Hey, you! Well what's the matter?
Was something coming to get you?
You look completely shattered.'

They had told everyone about my
plan,
they all pretended not to know.
When I hid under the table
they all pretended to go.

But really they hid in school as well
in corners and outside the door.
It was them that made the noises
and made the tables move on the
floor.

'So you're the one not scared?
Scared of nothing at all?
You're our hero,' they said.
'You up for staying for more?'

'No,' I said. 'No, no no no no.
I've had enough, more than enough.
I'm not doing this again,
I'm not doing any of this stuff.'

Cool School

Who put the cool in school?
Was it Dave the Dude,
was it Rick the Rude,
who put the cool in school?
Was it Buddy the Bad,
was it Sid the Sad,
who put the cool in school?

Sometimes I'm crazy
sometimes I'm lazy
sometimes I'm rough
sometimes I'm tough
but I didn't put the cool in school.

So who's got the ice?
Who's got the chill?
Who's got the freeze
to pump in and fill
my school and your school with
cool?

Thumb Pots

One day we did pottery.
We made thumb pots.

You take a chunk of clay.
You bash it and roll it and bash it.
You make it into a chunk the size of
a fist.

You stick your thumb in
and then keep turning it round
squeezing it with your fingers.

That's a thumb pot.

When I was finished
I put up my hand.
'Yes,' said Mr Baggs.
I said:
'I've finished my bum pot, sir.'

Everybody laughed
and I was sent out.

But I didn't mean to say bum pot.
I don't know why I said bum pot.

Outside the classroom door
I thought:
It was quite funny though.
Bum pot.

Handwriting

There's a handwriting competition.
'Everyone's got to go in for the
handwriting competition.'

'But, miss, I'm hopeless at
handwriting.
There's no point in my going in for
the handwriting competition.'

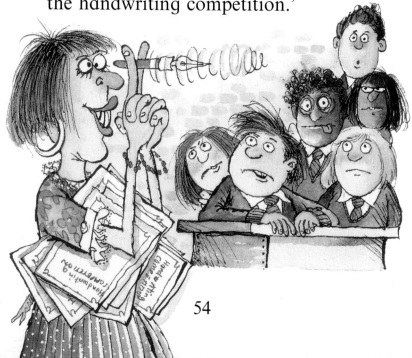

'Everyone's got to go in for the
handwriting competition.'

Miss gave us a booklet with lines
ruled across it.
There was a story on one side
and on the other was the space
where we had to write out the story
in our own handwriting.

55

'But, miss, I'm hopeless at
handwriting.
There's no point in my going in for
the handwriting competition.'

'Everyone's got to go in for the
handwriting competition.'

So I started writing.
And when I made the loop at the
top of the l's
or at the bottom of the g's
my pen blobbed.
All the loops filled up.

By the time I had finished
the whole page was covered in
blobs.

Miss came round to collect them up.
When she saw mine she said:
'Well, Michael,
there really wasn't much point in you
going in for the handwriting
competition,
was there?'